FIND YOUR WINE

KAYTIE NORMAN & NICK JOHNSON

Foreword

BY VICTORIA JAMES

Wine words can be scary— Pyrazines, Monoterpenes, Rotundone, Trichloroanisole. Even as an experienced sommelier, I often come across words in this business that intimidate the hell out of me. It took me years to verbalize what I was tasting in wine and learn how to recommend it to guests.

Along my path to becoming an expert, people didn't make it easy. When I asked a question, it was often answered with an even more complicated question (usually a rhetorical one). Words that seemed longer than necessary, and technical terms I couldn't even begin to imagine how to spell were sprinkled in for added oomph! These elite intellects made me feel like I would never understand wine properly.

Well, I was wrong. It took a while but I soon became the youngest sommelier in the country and now I'm a partner in a Michelin-starred restaurant group. I have won every possible award a sommelier can win, and titles many didn't think a sommelier could even earn. I am telling you this not to toot my own horn but because after all this, I finally realized a profound truth that others had kept secret: learning about wine can be easy and fun!

Find Your Wine will show you how to describe what you like, the most important part of drinking and enjoying wine. Imagine going into a record shop and not being able to say you like funky soul music or classic jazz. How would the clerk know what to recommend? If you can only describe the music you like as "cool" or "smooth," the clerk would have to do a lot of guessing and most likely you'd end up with something you only kind of like.

Getting your wine vocab together is just as important! Don't worry about memorizing esoteric laws governing canopy management; leave that to the sommeliers. Instead, figure out if you like Cabernet Franc or Merlot (or maybe both!) and what white goes well with roasted chicken. Learn about some classic pairings (Gewürztraminer and Muenster cheese are a dream together) and some not-so-classics (Sangiovese and watching *The Silence of the Lambs*). You soon will start having a much better time in restaurants and might even learn enough to impress your in-laws!

With solid advice from some of my favorite wine pros like Yannick Benjamin (super inspirational dude), Paul Grieco (really rad guy) and Kevin Zraly (the legend himself!), you are in good hands. This book will not only help you find your wine, but also your next wine and your *next* next wine. Cheers to that.

> ## "Anyone who tries to make you believe that he knows all about wines is obviously a fake."
>
> **—LEON D. ADAMS,**
> *The Commonsense Book of Wine*

Leon Adams was right. There are mind-boggling numbers of different grapes, methods, regions and winemakers in the world, and each one of these factors affects how a wine tastes, making it impossible to become an expert on every aspect of the good stuff. And if you're not fortunate enough to get paid to know a lot about wine, it can also make the idea of learning about it somewhat intimidating. Luckily, you don't have to be a master sommelier (a French title that basically means "professional wine person") to have a working knowledge of the basics or develop a sense of what you like and how to talk about it. You just need to pay attention to what you're drinking.

Unlike many other wine books, *Find Your Wine* isn't organized by region, which can be an overwhelming—and if we're being honest, pretty boring—way for casual drinkers to think about wine. Plus, if you're not a professional, you presumably don't really care how different kinds of soil affect your wine, nor do you want to get into the nitty-gritty of regional appellations (though it can be handy to know a little bit about those—see p. 14).

Instead, this primer on wine is divided by the major styles, which is more useful for picking something based on your mood or personal preference. Each style is introduced by a wine you've probably had before (or have at least heard of), and includes a few examples of less common wines that are made in a similar style—think of those as good jumping off points for trying something new.

Find Your Wine also addresses numerous questions people tend to have about wine: how to read a label,

the "proper" way to taste and drink wine, tips for choosing it, decanting it, storing it and pairing it with food—everything you need to know to confidently enjoy wine.

There's just one more thing to know before you dive in: Wine is weird. Because of all those factors we mentioned earlier, there are exceptions to just about everything. So drink with an open mind, ask your server or local shops questions about the specific wines you're buying, and try things you've never heard of—it's more fun that way. Cheers!

MEET THE EXPERTS

—

They're kind of a big deal.

YANNICK BENJAMIN

Yannick Benjamin is the Head Sommelier at the University Club and an Advanced Sommelier with the Court of Master Sommeliers. He has worked at Le Cirque, Oceana, Jean-Georges, Atlas, Felidia and Atelier at the Ritz-Carlton. Yannick has been recognized among *Wine Enthusiast*'s Top 40 Under 40 and was named Person of the Year by *New Mobility Magazine* in 2017.

> "I think the biggest issue that consumers have, particularly when they're getting into wine, is they're afraid of being judged. They're afraid of people looking down at them. And that, I think, you need to avoid."
> —Yannick Benjamin

PAUL GRIECO

Paul Grieco is a New York City-based sommelier and restaurateur. He has won two James Beard Awards, the first in 2002 for "Wine Service" (at Gramercy Tavern) and the second in 2012, for "Outstanding Wine, Beer or Spirits Professional." Paul is known for his acclaimed wine bar Terroir, whose brick & mortar location is in the Tribeca neighborhood of Manhattan.

> "You should never forget that wine is, at its heart, grape juice with alcohol. No more, no less. The intimidation factor is not an inherent part of the beverage; it's something that some have contrived over all of these centuries and surrounded this beverage with. Put that aside and just jump in and drink." —Paul Grieco

ADAM TEETER

Adam Teeter is the cofounder of *VinePair*, a site dedicated to making wine easy to understand. He was also a member of the winning team at the 2014 Left Bank Bordeaux Cup American Wine-Tasting Championship and holds an MBA from NYU Stern.

"No matter what it is, whether someone's giving you a Grand Cru Burgundy or someone's giving you a bottle of Kim Crawford Sauvignon Blanc, the biggest thing is whether you like it. And if you like it, then try to figure out what other wines taste like it so you can drink more wines that you like." —Adam Teeter

COURTNEY SCHIESSL

Courtney Schiessl is a Brooklyn-based wine journalist, educator and consultant who has held sommelier positions at some of New York's top restaurants. Her work has appeared in *Forbes*, *SevenFifty Daily*, *The SOMM Journal*, *The Tasting Panel Magazine* and *VinePair*, among other publications.

"When I was working as a sommelier, so many people were afraid to not know [about wine]. So just ask people who know more than you. Ask about the wine, ask about the grape, ask about the regions, and that way, slowly you'll learn more." —Courtney Schiessl

RUPAL SHANKAR

AKA "The Syrah Queen," Rupal Shankar is a popular wine writer (syrahqueen.com) and enthusiast who has met with wine makers around the globe. She has a WSET Advanced Certificate (Level 3) and has been awarded a certificate for French Wine Scholar by the French Wine Society.

"Explore wines and regions that you haven't heard of. I guarantee you they're gonna be good and they're gonna be at a really reasonable price point." —Rupal Shankar

KEVIN ZRALY

Kevin Zraly is the founder and instructor of the Windows on the World Wine School and author of multiple bestselling wine books, including *Windows on the World Complete Wine Course*. Notably among his achievements, he was the winner of the James Beard Award for Wine and Spirits Professional of the Year in 1993 and received the 2011 James Beard Lifetime Achievement Award.

"This is the golden age of wine in the history of the world. When I started it was only French wines. Today, Chile, Argentina, South Africa, Australia, New Zealand, the U.S.A., Italy, Spain; now [they all] produce great wine. There's just so much good stuff out there." —Kevin Zraly

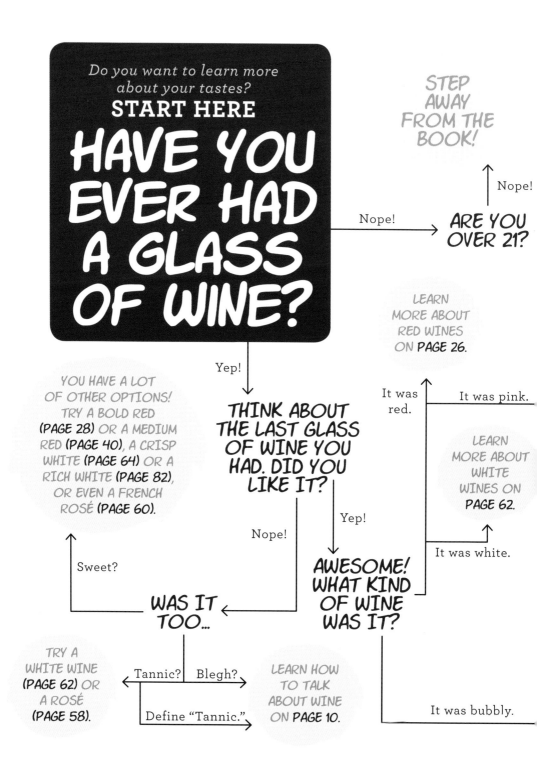

Do you want to learn more about your tastes?
START HERE

HAVE YOU EVER HAD A GLASS OF WINE?

Nope! →

STEP AWAY FROM THE BOOK!

↑ Nope!

ARE YOU OVER 21?

LEARN MORE ABOUT RED WINES ON **PAGE 26.**

Yep! ↓

THINK ABOUT THE LAST GLASS OF WINE YOU HAD. DID YOU LIKE IT?

It was red. ← It was pink.

LEARN MORE ABOUT WHITE WINES ON **PAGE 62.**

It was white. ↑

Yep! ↓

AWESOME! WHAT KIND OF WINE WAS IT?

YOU HAVE A LOT OF OTHER OPTIONS! TRY A BOLD RED **(PAGE 28)** OR A MEDIUM RED **(PAGE 40),** A CRISP WHITE **(PAGE 64)** OR A RICH WHITE **(PAGE 82),** OR EVEN A FRENCH ROSÉ **(PAGE 60).**

Nope! →

Sweet? ↑

WAS IT TOO...

TRY A WHITE WINE **(PAGE 62)** OR A ROSÉ **(PAGE 58).**

← Tannic?   Blegh? →

LEARN HOW TO TALK ABOUT WINE ON **PAGE 10.**

Define "Tannic." →

It was bubbly.

Do you want to learn more about how people buy and drink wine?

START HERE

DO YOU HAVE ANY WINE?

ep! →

Uhhh... →

PREPARE YOURSELF BY READING ABOUT WINE LABELS **(PAGE 12)**, APPELLATIONS **(PAGE 14)** AND GENERAL WINE WORDS **(PAGE 10)**.

↑
I don't know if I'm ready for that.

LET'S FIX THAT. LEARN MORE ABOUT BUYING AND ORDERING WINE ON **PAGE 16**.

Yep! ↓

LEARN MORE ABOUT ROSÉ ON **PAGE 58**.

IS IT A SPARKLING WINE?

Nope!

Yep!

LEARN MORE ABOUT SPARKLING WINES (AND HOW TO OPEN THEM) ON **PAGE 88**.

DO YOU NEED TO DECANT IT?

Define "decant." →

LEARN MORE ABOUT DECANTING ON **PAGE 18**.

I de-can't and I de-won't.
↓

LET'S GET TO DRINKING! LEARN THE "PROPER" WAY ON **PAGE 24**.

Hang on, I wanted to pair this wine with some food... →

NO PROBLEM! LEARN MORE ABOUT THAT ON **PAGE 22**. UNLESS YOU WERE THINKING DESSERT—THEN SEE **PAGE 94**.

WINE WORDS

We've covered all the basic vocabulary
you'll need for talking about wine.

ABV
Alcohol by volume. The majority of wines have an ABV between 10 and 15 percent.

According to **Kevin Zraly**, beginner wine drinkers should start with lower ABV wines—German bottles are often a safe bet. "It's like having lemonade with alcohol."

Acidic
The crisp quality in a wine that makes your mouth water. Low acidity wines are sometimes described as "round" or "soft."

Appellation
A designation given to a product made in a specific region.

Balance
The ratio of fruit and sugar to acidity and tannin in a wine.

Big
A wine with a lot of flavor that you taste all over your mouth. Fruit and tannins can both taste "big."

Blend
A wine that is made from multiple varieties of grapes.

Body
The "weight" of the wine on your palate. Big wines high in alcohol or sugar generally feel fuller in body, while more "delicate" high-acidity wines feel lighter.

Corked
A wine that has spoiled because of cork taint.

Creamy
Having a texture that is rich, like cream. Many oak-aged wines develop a creamy texture.

Dry
The opposite of sweet; a wine with little or no residual sugar. Wines range from dry and off-dry to semi-sweet and sweet.

Earthy
Sometimes considered the opposite of a fruity wine; "earthy" can mean minerality, or savory notes like mushrooms.

Fruity
AKA "fruit-forward," a wine that hits you in the face with sweet fruit smells. Note: Many dry wines are fruity.

Grippy
Strong tannins are

sometimes described as "grippy" because of how they cling to your mouth.

Jammy
Exactly what it sounds like: a red wine that is sweet with a bit of viscosity. Zinfandel, Grenache and Cab Franc are all likely to be described as jammy.

Minerality
There's no one accepted definition for this, but generally, a flavor or aroma that reminds you of stone.

As **Yannick Benjamin** puts it, "If you ever were a kid by a river and you took some river rocks and you were sucking on it, that would be a form of minerality." He also suggests chalk dust and that flinty aroma you get if you scrape two rocks together.

New World
Wines produced outside of Europe. These wines are generally labeled according to the grapes used to make them (e.g., California Chardonnay).

Old World
Wines produced in Europe. These wines are generally labeled according to the region where they were grown (e.g., Bordeaux).

According to **Paul Grieco**, the Old World has a particular reason for naming wines this way. "With every step you take, the belief is the soil changes and, therefore, what you are doing is honoring the soil. So when you go to Tuscany, you're not drinking Sangiovese—you're drinking Chianti. And when you take an hour trip down the Autostrade and you go to the hilltop town of Montalcino, you're not drinking Sangiovese, the same grape that's in Chianti; you're now drinking Brunello di Montalcino."

Residual Sugar
Sugar that exists in the wine after fermentation is complete—once the yeast has done its job turning sugar into alcohol and CO_2, any sugar left over is residual.

Spicy
Wine that has notes of spices like cinnamon, pepper, clove, etc.

Sweet
A wine with enough residual sugar that sweetness is the dominant feature. Dessert wines are generally sweet wines.

Tannins
The phenolic compounds in wine that leave a dry feeling in your mouth. These compounds come from the skins and seeds of the grape.

"You know when you bite into a grape and the skin is really thick? You're going to feel that little dryness around your lips and on your tongue. That's what the tannin is."
—Rupal Shankar

Tight
A wine that is not ready to drink, usually because of very high tannins. Swirling the wine in a glass or otherwise aerating it can help it "open up" so it's more enjoyable to drink.

READING A WINE LABEL
—

To get the basics down, let's look at these fairly simple labels.

NEW WORLD

1 PRODUCER OR NAME

Who made the wine (or in this case, a label the producer made). It's usually very prominent or written in small text along the top or bottom of the label.

2 REGION

Where the wine was made. As a rule of thumb, wine quality increases with region specificity. So if you're debating between two similarly priced bottles of Merlot and one says "Italy" while the other says "Veneto," go with the latter.

3 VINTAGE

The year the grapes were harvested.

NEW VS. OLD WORLD

There are three different ways of labeling wine: by grape variety, by region or just by making up a name. Most New World wines (from anywhere but Europe) are labeled by grape variety, while Old World (European) wines are labeled by region. If a wine is labeled by an original name, it might mean it contains an unusual blend of grapes which can't legally be labeled by region. You can usually find out more about these wines on the producer's website or simply by asking whoever is selling the wine—there's a pretty good chance they've tasted it. Don't be afraid to ask about regions or grapes you don't recognize, too!

OLD WORLD

VARIETY OR APPELLATION

Depending on whether the wine is New World or Old World, it will either list the kind of grape used or give more specific information about where the grapes were grown. You can look up the appellation to determine what kind of grapes are in the wine.

⑤ ABV

An acronym for Alcohol By Volume, this can be a good indicator of the kind of wine you're buying. Wines with less than 10 percent ABV tend to be lighter and sweeter, while higher ABVs often mean bolder and richer wine—and, for some, a higher chance for hangovers.

KNOW YOUR CLASSES

Your cheat sheet for French, Italian and Spanish wines.

Many countries have strict regulations for making wine based on the quality and types of the grapes used, the places where they were grown (known as appellations), how the wine is aged and more. Their wine is then labeled according to certain classifications. The higher the classification, the stricter the standards for making the wine. While a lower classification doesn't necessarily mean poor quality (especially in France, Italy and Spain), recognizing different classifications can help you understand why wines are priced differently and when to expect super high quality—and, if nothing else, which words on a label make a wine an impressive pick for your boss or a fancy party.

(Note: The U.S., home of Two-Buck Chuck and proud purveyors of aerosol processed cheese spread product, is not one of the countries with a quality-based hierarchy for its appellations. That being said, the U.S. does makes a lot of incredible wine, and the general rule still applies that the more specific the place on the label, the better the wine probably is.)

 ## FRANCE

Vin de France is the lowest classification, guaranteeing that at least the grapes were grown in France.

Vin de Pays (IGP, or Indication Géographique Protégée) is the mid-tier classification. These wines will tell you which French region they were made in.

Appellation d'Origine Contrôlée/Protégée (AOC/AOP) is the highest tier with the strictest regulations. Within AOC, certain terms will indicate even more requirements that the wine has to meet. "Premier Cru" and "Grand Cru" means extremely good quality, while "Villages" wines are usually a great way to drink very good wine without blowing your budget.

ITALY

Vino da Tavola, or just vino, is the most inexpensive category.

IGT, or Indicazione di Geografica Tipica, is a mid-tier classification, similar to France's IGP.

DOC, or Denominazione di Origine Controllata, is a stricter classification. DOC wines that are regularly proven to be of high quality are given the high status of a DOCG (Denominazione di Origine Controllata e Garantita) wine.

Note: Because they don't follow DOC rules regarding grapes, "Super Tuscans" are labeled IGT. Despite this, they're known to be high quality, expensive wines. Super Tuscans are always from Tuscany and tend to have original names.

EXTRA ITALIAN

Superiore
A higher minimum quality of grapes and minimum aging requirement.

Riserva
Wines that have been aged for a long time prior to release.

SPAIN

Vino de la Tierra (VT), or "wine of the land," is the most flexible category.

Vinos de Calidad con Indicación Geográfica (VC) are mid-tier wines, similar to an Italian IGT or French IGP.

Denominación de Origen (DO) wines are the next tier up, and on the same quality level as Vino de Pago (VP), a wine which, similarly to Super Tuscans, is of high quality but does not meet traditional standards.

Denominación de Origen Calificada (DOC) is Spain's highest classification. Only two regions of Spain produce wines in this category: Rioja and Priorat.

EXTRA SPANISH

Spanish wines have often been aged and are labeled to reflect that.

LITTLE TO NO AGING   A LOT OF AGING

| Joven | Crianza | Reserva | Gran Reserva |

3 STEPS TO BUYING BETTER WINE

—

Talk to someone who knows more than you do.

FIND A GOOD WINE STORE

Be it from word-of-mouth recommendations, online reviews or just checking out the stores in your neighborhood and seeing which one gives you the best vibe, having a good wine store with knowledgeable employees is key to trying a lot of good wines at a great price.

Really—Don't Be Afraid to Ask Questions

"We all had to start somewhere, so if you think it's the stupidest question in the world, then you need to ask it because it's probably the greatest question. And I think working with a real professional, someone who's passionate about wine, they are absolutely going to love it. That's what they're there for. They welcome those kinds of questions and you're not only going to get the proper glass of wine that you're looking for—you're going to feel enhanced. You're going to feel stimulated from all the knowledge you just learned from that question you were afraid to ask in the first place." **—Yannick Benjamin**

② ENGAGE IN CONVERSATION

Think of a wine shop employee like a cross between your hairdresser and a tour guide—good ones are people who you can trust, build a rapport with and help you discover new things. And remember, there are literally thousands of different producers, regions and kinds of wine, which makes it virtually impossible to be familiar with everything you see in any given shop unless you work there, so there's really no shame in asking questions.

By the Glass

If you're still trying to learn what kinds of wines you like, a restaurant or wine bar is not the cheapest place to do it. That being said, you can probably talk to the bartender, server or sommelier about what you like and sample a few different wines before settling on a glass.

According to Paul Grieco, "You're going to have to make two statements to that person. 'These are the types of wines I've had in the past and I really enjoy, and I would like something like that,' or 'These are the things that I don't like,' or 'I'm in a summery mood tonight and I would like a summery type of wine,' however you want to say it. That would be No. 1, and No. 2 would be your budget. And with those two pieces of information, the beverage director, the somm, the server—whoever it is—can then go about their job, which they really love to do, and find something that's going to rock your world."

③ THERE'S AN APP FOR THAT

Asking questions of people who are passionate about wine and who are dedicated to helping you find something great in your price range is ideal, but if you're in a rush or all the shop workers are busy, there are apps that can scan a wine label (or even a wine list) and give you reviews, average prices and suggested pairings—Rupal Shankar suggests *Vivino*, one of the more popular wine apps.

You Probably Shouldn't Order Wine at a Bar

Unless you're at a wine bar, that is. According to Kevin Zraly: "At a bar, the last thing I'm going to do is order a glass of wine because they're just going to find the lowest common denominator—something that looks red, might not even be red but it looks red. As my girlfriend says, 'If I'm going to have one glass of wine a day, it's going to be good.' That should be a philosophy."

WHEN YOU CAN (AND CAN'T) DECANT

If you do, first stand the bottle upright to let any sediment settle.

Decanting serves two purposes: to separate out any sediment in the bottom of the bottle and to aerate the wine, which can help emphasize its flavors and aromas. Older red wines naturally produce sediment which is unpleasant to drink, so if it's at least 5 years old, decanting is probably a good idea.

You *can* decant any wine—the exposure to oxygen rounds out the flavors and makes it more pleasing to most people's palates—but high tannin wines (i.e., wines that really dry out your mouth—see examples to the right) benefit the most from decanting. Decant as little as five minutes or up to two hours. Be careful about decanting longer—you don't want to let your wine become oxidized.

Can't decant because you can't find your decanter? Try using a wide-bottomed iced tea pitcher.

TRY DECANTING

- Syrah
- Barolo
- Brunello di Montalcino
- Chianti
- Nebbiolo
- Cabernet Sauvignon
- Tempranillo
- Montepulciano

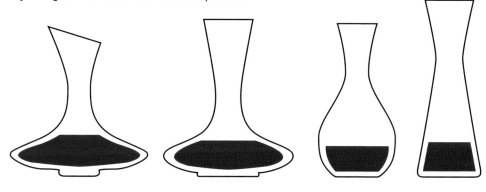

Decanters come in a lot of **funky shapes,** but you should probably just pick one that's easy to clean.

If you get your hands on a really old wine (think more than 15 years), be careful with decanting. According to the "Syrah Queen," Rupal Shankar, extremely old wines are very fragile and can easily get too much oxygen. "When a wine gets older, the top-off level tends to drop, meaning that if you look at a new bottle of wine, it's filled pretty much to the top," she says. "And then over time, that wine starts to evaporate because of oxygen exposure, so adding more oxygen to it actually hurts the wine." In cases like these, keep the wine in the bottle but leave it standing upright for at least an hour before serving—this will let the sediment fall to the bottom so you can avoid pouring most of it into the glass.

STORING YOUR WINE

Time to break out the wine rack!

As a rule of thumb, any wine that costs less than $30 is meant to be consumed within two to three years of being bottled, and the majority of more expensive bottles are still meant to be enjoyed within five years. Storing those bottles is pretty simple: Put them somewhere the temperature won't fluctuate dramatically (next to the oven is not a great idea) and keep the following tips in mind.

1 KEEP IT COOL

Around 55 degrees F is ideal, though anything between 45–65 degrees F is generally OK. You can also store unopened wine in your refrigerator for up to two months.

2 AVOID THE SUN

The sun's UV rays are not good for your wine, so make sure it's being stored in a shady spot.

3 STICK TO THE SIDE

If your wine is sealed with a real cork (as opposed to a synthetic one or a screw cap), store it on its side—the wine will keep the cork from drying out.

Storing Opened Wine

How long will that leftover wine last? It depends. According to Courtney Schiessl: "Always cork it back up or put a stopper on it and keep it in your fridge whether it's a red or a white because it keeps for longer. Most light, delicate white wines you should probably drink within three days; the bolder, richer, more tannic and more structured reds you can keep probably for five days." After that, feel free to cook with it—it's effectively turning to vinegar.

Only about 1 percent of bottles produced are suitable for aging long-term.

WINE PAIRING CHEAT SHEET

You can see more specific food and wine pairings on each grape's bio, but remember these fast rules when you need to make a quick call about which wine to grab for dinner. And remember—you can always drink wine on its own. And on your own.

RED WINES

Most red wines are somewhat bitter. They go well with bold meats and are balanced well with fat. Generally avoid pairing a medium or bold red wine with fish.

The "Perfect Pairing"

"It's up to you; that's the beauty of wine and food pairings. You have this moment where you try a wine with a dish you're having and if it makes the wine better and the dish better, that's the perfect pairing."
—**Adam Teeter**

Most unoaked white wines, sparkling wines and rosés are acidic. Remember: Acidic means mouth-watering. With tart citrus or earthy mineral notes, these kinds of wines are refreshing and light, and usually go well with a similarly light meal.

According to Paul Grieco, "Rule of thumb, if I am to give rule of thumb for [wine pairings], is something that a lot of chefs say when they're trying to compose a dish: 'If it grows together, it goes together.'" In other words, if you want to have a great wine and food pairing without having to really think about it, choose a wine from the same region your dish is from (like an Italian Nebbiolo with a truffle risotto, or duck confit with a bottle from Bordeaux) and it's virtually guaranteed to be an excellent match.

OAKED WHITE WINES

Most oaked white wines are full-bodied and a little creamy. Oak-aged white wines often pick up spicy notes, not unlike bourbon. They go well with richer dishes and buttery seafood.

Don't Overthink It

It's not a cardinal sin to open whatever you have on hand to go with your food, especially for a casual lunch or dinner. (Or brunch or breakfast—we're not judging.) Great wine and food pairings bring out delicious nuances in one another, but your meal will almost definitely still be good if you wing it.

TASTING YOUR WINE

While you don't have to do anything to your wine before you drink it, it's helpful to understand why some people go through a bit of a routine before taking their first sip.

① EXAMINE THE COLOR

Tilt the glass at a 45-degree angle and look from above. (This view is shown on the "Tasting Notes" pages.) You'll be able to tell the "intensity" of the wine by how opaque it is and whether the pigment extends all the way to the edges. The darker a red wine, the more likely it is to be high tannin—red wines get their color and tannin from contact with grape skins. With white wines, a bolder color usually indicates a fuller body (and probably oak-aging).

② SWIRL THE WINE

Swirling wine in its glass adds a little bit of oxygen to the wine, rounding out its flavors, extracting its aromas and helping it "open up" and be more pleasant to drink.

According to Adam Teeter, "glassware is bulls**t"— kind of. You don't need specialty Merlot or Chardonnay glasses to enjoy those varietals (and most casual drinkers won't notice the difference), but if you want to learn more about wine, you should at least be drinking out of a wine glass. As Teeter explains it, "You want the bowl to allow you to swirl the wine and allow the oxygen to open it up. I think of the sort of Italian trattoria tumbler wine glasses, they're great for really casual weeknight sipping."

3 SMELL THE WINE

You might feel a little silly sticking your nose in the wine glass, but it's true what they say: taste is closely tied to smell. Smelling your wine prepares your brain for what you're about to drink and gives you a chance to show off how good you are at identifying scents. Also, smelling the wine will give you a heads up about whether the bottle has cork taint, also known as being "corked."

About 5 percent of wine bottles with natural corks have "cork taint," meaning a fungus in the cork has made your wine a bit funky. The telltale signs of cork taint are a scent like wet cardboard or wet dog. Not sure if you smell that? Rupal Shankar also recommends sniffing the cork of the bottle, where the scent is probably stronger. Corked wine is pretty dull, without any fruit flavors. If your wine is corked, bring it back to the shop where you bought it—they'll probably let you exchange it for a new bottle.

Improving Your Sense of Smell

Being able to detect every scent in your wine isn't terribly important, but identifying more common flavors can be useful for figuring out your own preferences. If you do want to get better at it, just pay more attention when you're smelling and tasting things. Sommelier Yannick Benjamin says, "If you're in a flower market or a farmers market, just take the time and smell things that are around and taste if you can. If you're at Whole Foods, if they have free samples, take the time to taste that. It's just a matter of building that vocabulary."

4 SIP THE WINE

There's nothing left to do but drink it and decide whether you like it! Whether you do or don't like it, it's useful to try to figure out why—that way you can use that information to figure out your tastes and start to recognize what different wine styles are like. Is it sweet? Fruity? Smoky? Is it light-bodied like skim milk, or fuller-bodied like cream? You can also pay attention to what it does to your mouth. If it dries out, it's high in tannins; if it makes your mouth water, it's more acidic.

Tasting Tip

It's easy to think fruity wines are always sweet since the fruit we eat is usually sweet. But when it comes to wine, this isn't always the case. If you have a hard time telling, Courtney Schiessl has a trick for picking out fruity wines that aren't actually sweet: "If you stick the tip of your tongue into the wine, there's no actual sugar there; it's just the flavor of sweet cherries and things like that. So when I'm teaching wine classes, I have all of my students put just the tip of their tongue in the wine and we all look like idiots together."

RED WINE

Featuring dark fruit flavors (like berries and stone fruit) and a fair amount of bitter tannins, dry red wine has been linked to a number of health benefits, including a decreased risk of heart disease, according to a study from the Israel Institute of Technology. It's also straight-up delicious.

Red wine gets its color—and tannins—by fermenting the juices of red grapes together with their skins.

During fermentation, yeast eats sugar and produces alcohol. Most red wines are fermented until all the sugar is gone, making a dry (not sweet) wine.

To bring medium or bold reds down to a cool room temp, place them in the fridge for 45 minutes or in the freezer for 5–10 minutes. If the wine tastes harsh and it's hard to detect the fruit flavors, it got a bit too cold—let it warm up a few degrees before enjoying.

BOLD REDS

The darkest and often most tannic of wines, bold reds are usually sipped slowly or alongside a fatty meal—classically a juicy steak. They're best served at room temperature, though room temperature in the wine world is a bit cooler than most of us are used to: 60–65 degrees F. Examples of bold reds include:

Aglianico	Mourvèdre	Syrah (p. 34)
Cabernet Sauvignon (p. 28)	Nero d'Avola	Tempranillo (p. 36)
Malbec (p. 30)	Pinotage (p. 38)	Zinfandel (p. 32)

MEDIUM REDS

Medium-bodied red wines are often a little more "complex" than light reds, with more pronounced flavors, acidity and tannins. They should be served at the same cool room temperature as bold reds. Examples of medium reds include:

Barbera	Grenache (p. 48)	Nebbiolo (p. 46)
Cabernet Franc (p. 42)	Merlot (p. 40)	Sangiovese (p. 44)

LIGHT REDS

Lighter in body, color and tannins, light red wines are best served slightly chilled (~55 degrees F). This is about 15 degrees less than room temperature, so toss them in the fridge for an hour or in the freezer for 20 minutes. Examples of light reds include:

Blaufränkisch	Pinot Noir (p. 50)	Zweigelt (p. 56)
Dolcetto	Schiava (p. 54)	
Gamay (p. 52)	Valpolicella	

CABERNET SAUVIGNON

—

CABERNET SAUVIGNON is the most-planted wine grape on earth, and is also recognized as playing a large role in Bordeaux's "left bank" blends.

PRIMARY CHARACTERISTICS

FRUIT *black cherry, black currant, blackberry*

OTHER *black pepper, tobacco, licorice, vanilla, violet*

TANNIN *medium*

ACIDITY *medium*

PAIRINGS

This wine's earthy and savory aspects position it well alongside very savory foods.

TRY IT WITH

Marinated steak

A veggie burger

Your in-laws

THE COMPOUND METHOXYPYRAZINE IS THE REASON CABS SMELL LIKE BLACK PEPPER AND CURRANTS.

Cabernet Sauvignon produced in **Bordeaux** is less fruity and more earthy. For a good introduction to a left bank Bordeaux, look for a bottle from the Médoc region.

California Cabernet Sauvignon is generally more fruity and sports a higher ABV. There are many regions (including but not limited to Napa) making great Cab Sauv in California.

MALBEC

—

MALBEC is generally a more affordable choice than Cabernet Sauvignon, while still offering a full body and a lot of fruit.

PRIMARY CHARACTERISTICS

FRUIT *dark berries, black cherry, pomegranate, plum*

OTHER *dark chocolate, coffee, leather, black pepper*

TANNIN *medium*

ACIDITY *medium*

PAIRINGS

Malbec's softer tannins means it pairs well with milder flavors. Avoid bitter greens, broccoli and vinegar.

TRY IT WITH

A blue cheese burger

Peppered flank steak

A hard-boiled mystery

PRIOR TO PROHIBITION IN THE U.S., MALBEC WAS A POPULAR CHOICE FOR MAKING JUG WINE.

Malbec grown in **Argentina** is large-bodied with lots of fruit. For some of the best examples, look for "Mendoza" on the label—a region near the Andes famous for its Malbec.

Malbec grown in **France** is typically drier, with slightly higher acidity. If you see the region "Cahors" on a label, that's (mostly) French Malbec.

ZINFANDEL

—

Not to be confused with White Zin, which is a sweeter, rosé-style wine, **ZINFANDEL** was made extremely popular by winemakers in California, who produce a lot of the jammy, higher-ABV wine.

PRIMARY CHARACTERISTICS

FRUIT   *jam, blueberry, cherry*

OTHER   *black pepper, licorice*

TANNIN *medium to medium-high*

ACIDITY *medium to medium-high*

PAIRINGS

As a sweeter red wine, Zinfandel is great alongside heavily spiced foods.

TRY IT WITH

Japanese curry

Manchego cheese

A snow day

RED AND WHITE ZINS ARE THE SAME GRAPE MADE IN EXTREMELY DIFFERENT STYLES.

When buying Zinfandel, check the **ABV**. Bolder and spicier Zins will be about 16 percent, while lighter ones will be closer to 13 percent.

Zinfandel is largely made in

California

though some bottles can be found from

Puglia, Italy

where the grape is called "Primitivo."

SYRAH

—

Also known as **SHIRAZ** in Australia, and the dominant grape of the northern Rhône region in France, **SYRAH** is one of the darkest red wines and has a high amount of health-benefiting antioxidants.

PRIMARY CHARACTERISTICS

FRUIT   *blackberry, blueberry, boysenberry*

OTHER   *pepper, tobacco, clove*

TANNIN *medium-high*

ACIDITY *medium-high*

PAIRINGS

Syrah goes especially well with <u>meat,</u> but you can drink it alongside almost any food.

TRY IT WITH

Grilled lamb

Stinky cheese

A backyard barbecue

SYRAH IS A DIFFERENT GRAPE THAN PETITE SIRAH, WHICH MAKES A VERY JUICY WINE.

Syrah from

Italy & **France**

tends to have more acidity and herbaceous aromas. Syrah can also have distinctive olive notes when it grows in cooler climates like these.

Syrah from the

Americas

& **Australia**

tends to be fruitier and spicier. You may even smell eucalyptus on some Australian Shiraz.

TEMPRANILLO

—

This bold grape is Spain's favorite, and is the primary varietal used to produce the country's most famous wine, **RIOJA**.

PRIMARY CHARACTERISTICS

FRUIT *plum, cherry, dried fig, tomato*

OTHER *tobacco, leather, clove, vanilla*

TANNIN *medium-high*

ACIDITY *medium-low*

PAIRINGS

When you're about to settle into a <u>hearty meal,</u> pull out a bottle of Tempranillo.

TRY IT WITH

Lasagna

Jamón serrano

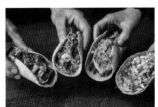
Taco Tuesday

THIS GRAPE RIPENS EARLIER THAN MOST SPANISH GRAPES, HENCE ITS NAME: *TEMPRANO* MEANS "EARLY."

New World Tempranillo from

U.S. & **Argentina** & **Mexico**

tends to have more fruit flavors and fewer earthy notes.

Tempranillo from **Spain** is known for its balance of fruity and earthy flavors.

PINOTAGE

—

A grape that was bred from Pinot Noir and Cinsault
(referred to as "Hermitage" in South Africa, hence the name),
this dense wine can be tricky to produce well.

PRIMARY CHARACTERISTICS

FRUIT   *plum, dark berries, red bell pepper*

OTHER   *smoke, rooibos, bacon*

TANNIN *high*

ACIDITY *low*

PAIRINGS

This dark red wine
stands up well to
heavily spiced foods
and hearty barbecue.

TRY IT WITH

Barbecue ribs

South African biryani

A camping trip

IN SOUTH AFRICA, THE SECOND SATURDAY OF OCTOBER IS PINOTAGE DAY.

Pinotage is rarely planted outside of **South Africa** and is sometimes used as part of the country's "Cape" blend (along with Cabernet Sauvignon, Merlot and others).

Pinotage is making a comeback after years as a "bulk" or "value" wine, with more and more high quality examples coming to market. The regions **Stellenbosch** and **Paarl** on the label are good indicators for quality.

MERLOT

—

Tasting of red fruits and boasting a soft finish and easy tannins, **MERLOT** is an accessible wine that's a safe choice for most occasions.

PRIMARY CHARACTERISTICS

FRUIT   *plum, black cherry, raspberry*

OTHER   *cedar, tobacco, graphite, mocha, vanilla, clove*

TANNIN *medium*

ACIDITY *medium*

PAIRINGS

Because of its medium tannins and acidity, Merlot pairs well with most foods except flakey white fish. The subtle flavors of a Merlot would also be lost if drunk alongside a spicy dish.

TRY IT WITH

Roasted
pork tenderloin

Chicken
cacciatore

A Netflix
binge

MERLOT IS THE DOMINANT GRAPE IN BORDEAUX'S "RIGHT BANK" RED WINE BLENDS.

Merlots from cool climates like

France & **Italy**

& **Chile**

tend to have more minerality and notes of tobacco.

Merlots from hot climates like

Argentina & **Australia**

& **California**

tend to have more notes of cocoa, mocha and berries. If you need a wine to drink with chocolate, these are good bets.

CABERNET FRANC

—

This grape is often used in blends, though you can find some excellent single-varietal bottles of **CAB FRANC.**

PRIMARY CHARACTERISTICS

FRUIT *strawberry, peppers, plum*

OTHER *licorice, tobacco*

TANNIN *medium-high*

ACIDITY *medium-high*

PAIRINGS

Because of its tannin and acidity levels, Cab Franc pairs well with a wide variety of foods but it really shines when paired with fresh herbs.

TRY IT WITH

Herbed chicken

Spiced cranberry sauce

A crisp autumn stroll

PSST: IT'S PRONOUNCED CABERNET "FRONK," NOT "FRANK."

More expensive, aging-worthy Cab Francs are produced in **France's Loire Valley**, especially in the Chinon, Bourgueil and Saumur regions.

Look for value bottles of Cab Franc from

Chile & **New York** & **California**

SANGIOVESE

—

This grape is the key component of Brunello di Montalcino, a famously spendy Italian red. For a less pricey bottle, look for Vino Nobile di Montepulciano or Chianti, both of which must be made with at least 70 percent **SANGIOVESE**.

PRIMARY CHARACTERISTICS

FRUIT *cherry, plum, tomato*

- -

OTHER *leather, brick, smoke*

- -

TANNIN *high*

- -

ACIDITY *high*

PAIRINGS

A savory wine, Sangiovese pairs well with lots of foods, but especially herbs and tomatoes.

TRY IT WITH

Spaghetti
bolognese

An Italian
cheese board

A viewing of
The Silence of the Lambs

THE NAME SANGIOVESE IS DERIVED FROM LATIN AND MEANS "BLOOD OF JOVE." YUM.

Old World Sangiovese is grown in

Italy & **Corsica** ↗

where it can be known by many names, including Morellino, Prugnolo, Nielluccio and more.

New World Sangiovese is mostly made in

Argentina & **California**

& **Washington**

NEBBIOLO

—

This red grape is famous for its place in **BAROLO** and **BARBARESCO** (two very good, very expensive wines), but it can also be found in more affordable bottles.

PRIMARY CHARACTERISTICS

FRUIT *cherry, raspberries*

- -

OTHER *rose, leather, anise*

- -

TANNIN *high*

- -

ACIDITY *high*

PAIRINGS

Unsurprisingly, this Italian grape is known for being paired with classic Italian foods.

TRY IT WITH

Braciole

Hard, salty cheese

A meeting with the Don
(or, you know, your CEO)

THE NAME NEBBIOLO COMES FROM THE ITALIAN *NEBBIA*, MEANING "FOG."

To sample Nebbiolo without paying for Barolo or Barbaresco, look for a bottle from the

Langhe region of **Italy**

or really branch out and try one from

Mexico   or   **Australia**

If you need a classic example of **"grippy tannins,"** take a sip of Nebbiolo to immediately understand what this term means.

GRENACHE

—

This hardy, versatile grape is grown in warm climates all over the world, from Chile to China.

PRIMARY CHARACTERISTICS

FRUIT *raspberry, black cherry, strawberry*

- -

OTHER *anise, tobacco, cinnamon*

- -

TANNIN *medium*

- -

ACIDITY *medium*

PAIRINGS

A spicy Grenache goes especially well with spicy foods.

TRY IT WITH

Moroccan tagine

Spanish chorizo

A night of salsa dancing

GRENACHE IS OFTEN FOUND IN BLENDS FROM THE SOUTH OF FRANCE, LIKE CÔTES-DU-RHÔNE.

American Grenache is fruit forward, with scents of licorice and flowers.

French Grenache & **Spanish** "Garnacha"

are both more herbal, with the French tending to be smokier.

PINOT NOIR

—

PINOT NOIR grapes are notoriously difficult to grow—that's why a good bottle of Pinot is often pricier than similar red wines.

PRIMARY CHARACTERISTICS

FRUIT *cranberry, raspberry, cherry*

- -

OTHER *vanilla, clove, mushroom, violet*

- -

TANNIN *medium-low*

- -

ACIDITY *medium-high*

PAIRINGS

Pinot Noir is known for pairing well with a wide range of foods. Thanks to its bright acidity, it can work with rich or light fare.

TRY IT WITH

Roasted mushrooms

Baked salmon

A potluck dinner

FRANCE'S BURGUNDY WINE IS MADE WITH 100 PERCENT PINOT NOIR, WHILE WHITE BURGUNDY IS CHARDONNAY.

French Pinot Noir tends to be earthy and light.

Italian Pinot Nero has a similar profile, with a bit more smoke and spice.

California Pinot Noir is bigger and fruitier.

Oregon Pinot Noir is a bit lighter and more tart.

GAMAY

—

GAMAY is famously made in Beaujolais, France, where it is (in)famous for its Nouveau style—the wines are aged for less than two months. To put this in perspective, most wines are aged for at least six months.

PRIMARY CHARACTERISTICS

FRUIT *raspberry, cherry, cranberry*

- -

OTHER *mushroom, smoke, banana, bubblegum*

- -

TANNIN *low*

- -

ACIDITY *high*

PAIRINGS

Known to be light and refreshing, Beaujolais is extra enjoyable when lightly chilled and served alongside just about anything.

TRY IT WITH

Fried chicken tacos   Seared tuna   Thanksgiving leftovers

"I'M NOT A FAN OF BEAUJOLAIS NOUVEAU, BUT A BIG FAN OF BEAUJOLAIS." —KEVIN ZRALY, WHO SUGGESTS THE MORGON AND FLEURIE VILLAGES FOR "UNBELIEVABLE WINES" UNDER $20.

Because it has barely been aged, **Beaujolais Nouveau** is a juicy light wine that's extremely easy to drink, but it also has a much shorter shelf life than most wines—after only six months you'll start to notice the fruit fading and the acidity going flat. Drink fast!

Top tier bottles of **"Cru" Beaujolais** are aged for much longer and develop much more complex and varied flavor profiles. Some of the best wines (like Morgon or Moulin-à-Vent) can be aged for years in the cellar—you can take your time with these.

SCHIAVA

—

This light, floral red wine is known for its candy-like flavor and for being a good red to drink in the summertime—if we didn't know better, we'd think it was rosé.

PRIMARY CHARACTERISTICS

FRUIT *strawberry, cherry*

OTHER *bubblegum, rose, violet, smoke*

TANNIN *low*

ACIDITY *medium*

PAIRINGS

Crisp and refreshing, this wine is perfect for drinking by itself or for adding some acidity to rich foods.

TRY IT WITH

Summer sausage

Fresh brie

A trashy book by the beach

SCHIAVA IS MOSTLY GROWN IN ALTO ADIGE, AN ITALIAN REGION BORDERING GERMANY.

In **Germany**, this grape goes by the name Trollinger.

In northern **Italy**, the grape is referred to as Vernatsch.

ZWEIGELT
—

This light and tart Austrian wine can be served chilled, making it an excellent warm-weather red.

PRIMARY CHARACTERISTICS

FRUIT *cherry, raspberry*

OTHER *cinnamon, peppercorn*

TANNIN *low*

ACIDITY *medium-high*

PAIRINGS

Because of its low tannin level, Zweigelt pairs especially well with light meats and fish.

TRY IT WITH

Pad thai

Huevos rancheros

An outdoor movie screening

THIS GRAPE WAS ORIGINALLY CALLED "ROTBURGER." THANKFULLY, THE NAME CHANGED TO HONOR ITS CREATOR, FRITZ ZWEIGELT.

Austria's cooler temperatures tend to produce lighter wines with higher acidity. Keep an eye out for bottles sealed with a red-white-red striped capsule on top—the Austrian government's seal of quality.

Zweigelt can be **lightly carbonated**, making it extra refreshing. It can also be made into a very high-end dessert wine.

ROSÉ WINE

This summertime favorite is everywhere for a reason—
the easy-drinking wine is absolutely delicious.

TAVEL   TEMPRANILLO   PROVENCE   SANGIOVESE

Rosé is (usually) not made by mixing red wine with white wine. That method is generally frowned upon, unless you're making rosé Champagne. The most common way to make rosé is to let the grape skins sit in the grape juice for 2 to 20 hours. The longer the skins stay in, the darker the wine becomes.

Rosé is made all over the world. France corners the market on rosé, but bottles are being made just about everywhere. Other big producers are Spain, Italy and the U.S., though rosé can also be found from places like Chile, Uruguay, Germany and Australia.

Generally speaking, rosé isn't meant to be aged long-term. There are rare bottles that are exceptions to this rule (like the deeply-colored Tavel and Bandol rosés), but most rosé should be consumed within a year or two of its release.

Rosé can be made from just about any red wine grape, and even some whites. There are more popular varietals and blends, though. Grenache, Sangiovese, Mourvèdre, Cinsault, Carignan, Pinot Noir and Syrah are all traditional choices. The grapes used can tell you a lot about what to expect—for example, Syrah and Grenache are widely used for spice and depth, while Cinsault usually adds refreshing watermelon notes to rosé.

It's not just for summer. If you really love rosé, there's no reason to only drink it when the weather is warm. High-acid wines like rosé are great for cutting through rich dishes, and some rosés have cranberry notes that are great for complementing holiday food. And obviously, a bottle of rosé Champagne is perfect for ringing in the new year. Just ask your local wine shop for recommendations!

FRENCH ROSÉ

The most popular **ROSÉ** from the south of France is labeled as Provence, Languedoc-Roussillon or Pays d'Oc.

PRIMARY CHARACTERISTICS

FRUIT *strawberry, raspberry, watermelon*

- -

OTHER *rose petals, minerals*

- -

TANNIN *low*

- -

ACIDITY *medium-high*

PAIRINGS

This crisp, dry rosé goes wonderfully with just about any classic summer fare.

TRY IT WITH

Grilled summer vegetables

Bánh mì

Playing hooky

BECAUSE IT'S NOT AGED VERY LONG, ROSÉ IS USUALLY A BUDGET-FRIENDLY OPTION.

Rosé from the Loire Valley is made from Cabernet Franc, Gamay and Pinot Noir—look for the latter in the excellent bottles of Sancerre rosé. Bordeaux rosé made from Cabernet Sauvignon and Merlot grapes tends to have a bit more body and fruit.

In Italy, rosé is labelled as rosato.

In Spain and other Spanish-speaking countries, it's referred to as rosado.

The grapes used will typically reflect what grows well in these warmer climates, producing rosé that is commonly darker in color and richer in body.

WHITE WINE

Usually bursting with citrus or tropical fruit flavors, white wines can range from light and crisp to full-bodied, creamy and oaky. No matter the style, they're best served cold.

Because white grape juices aren't usually fermented with their skins, white wines are very low in tannins.

If you see a bottle or wine list that mentions "orange" wine, this is most likely white wine that has been fermented with the skins—essentially the white wine version of rosé. They're usually aged in cement or ceramic vessels and have a slightly funky, earthy taste, along with sour and nutty notes.

CRISP WHITES

Light in body with refreshing notes of citrus (and sometimes flowers or herbs), crisp white wines are best served chilled, at 45–50 degrees F. From room temperature, this means storing the wine in the fridge for 2½ hours or in the freezer for 25 minutes. Examples of crisp whites include:

Albariño (p. 68)	Grüner Veltliner (p. 70)	Sauvignon Blanc (p. 66)
Assyrtiko	Pinot Blanc	Vermentino (p. 72)
Chardonnay (unoaked)	Pinot Grigio (p. 64)	

AROMATIC WHITES

These wines are bursting with floral aromas and often on the sweeter side, best served at the same temperature as crisp whites. If that doesn't sound like your thing, try sipping them alongside something spicy or salty to balance the sweetness. Or just drink something else. Examples of aromatic whites include:

Chenin Blanc (p. 80)	Moscato (p. 76)	Torrontés
Gewürztraminer (p. 78)	Riesling (p. 74)	

RICH WHITES

With a full body and lots of warm notes from being aged in oak barrels, these can seem more decadent than other white wines. Serve them at 50–55 degrees F—about 2 hours in the fridge or 20 minutes in the freezer. Examples of rich whites include:

Chardonnay (oaked) (p. 82)	Sémillon (p. 84)	Viognier (p. 86)
Marsanne	Trebbiano	White Rioja

PINOT GRIGIO

Also known as Pinot Gris, **PINOT GRIGIO** is one of the most popular wines in America.

PRIMARY CHARACTERISTICS

FRUIT *citrus, green apple, pear, white peach*

OTHER *almond, honey, saline, clove, ginger*

ACIDITY *medium-high to high*

PAIRINGS

Because of its zesty acidity, Pinot Grigio pairs well with green vegetables and lighter fish or chicken dishes.

TRY IT WITH

Grilled tilapia

Roasted chicken

Cocktail attire

PINOT GRIGIO IS GREAT FOR COOKING, AS ARE OTHER CRISP WHITES.

Pinot Grigio from

Austria & Hungary

Lombardy and Veneto in Italy

tends to be more minerally and dry.

Pinot Grigio from

Tuscany & Australia & and Sicily in Italy Chile

tends to be fruitier.

SAUVIGNON BLANC

—

Meaning "Wild White," **SAUVIGNON BLANC** became famous for its popularity in Bordeaux and the Loire Valley in France.

PRIMARY CHARACTERISTICS

FRUIT *lime, green apple, Asian pear, kiwi, passionfruit*

OTHER *green bell pepper, basil, jalapeño, tarragon, lemongrass*

ACIDITY *medium-high to high*

PAIRINGS

This fresh wine and its green flavor pairs well with similar green herbs. If your dish has rosemary, basil or cilantro, it'll make a great partner for this wine.

TRY IT WITH

Fish tacos

Fried chicken

A garden stroll

OAK-AGED SAUVIGNON BLANC FROM THE U.S.
IS OFTEN LABELED "FUMÉ BLANC."

Sauvignon Blanc from Sancerre is famous for its crisp minerality and sharp acidity, but just across the Loire River in Pouilly-Fumé the grape is produced in a fuller, slightly softer style.

Northern New Zealand makes Sauvignon Blanc with more tropical flavors, while the south produces more acidic styles.

ALBARIÑO

—

ALBARIÑO is a refreshing and citrusy pale white wine, similar to Pinot Grigio or a dry Riesling.

PRIMARY CHARACTERISTICS

FRUIT *lemon, grapefruit, honeydew*

OTHER *saline, beeswax*

ACIDITY *medium-high to high*

PAIRINGS

Albariño's high acidity and citrus flavors make it an excellent choice for seafood dishes.

TRY IT WITH

Paella

Coconut lemongrass mussels

A poolside nap

PORTUGUESE BOTTLES MAY BE LABELED AS
ALVARINHO OR CAINHO BRANCO.

Albariño is mostly produced in

Spain

&

Portugal

You can also find Albariño from

California & Argentina

& New Zealand

GRÜNER VELTLINER

—

Literally translated as "green wine of Veltlin," this white wine has—you guessed it—a pale green hue. Look how good at wine you are!

PRIMARY CHARACTERISTICS

FRUIT *lemon, lime, grapefruit*

OTHER *white pepper, green pepper*

ACIDITY *high*

PAIRINGS

Grüner Veltliner works well alongside rich, spicy foods.

TRY IT WITH

Wiener schnitzel

Kung pao chicken

A lake house vacation

WHEN DRINKING WITH AUSTRIANS, CLINK YOUR GLASSES, MAKE EYE CONTACT AND SAY, "PROST!"

Grüner Veltliner is mostly grown in

Austria
(look for that red-white-red cap),

but you can also find bottles from other Old World countries such as

Hungary & Czech Republic

New World examples hail from the

U.S. & Australia

& New Zealand

VERMENTINO

This Italian white wine is similar to Sauvignon Blanc, but less name recognition means it generally has a lower price tag.

PRIMARY CHARACTERISTICS

FRUIT *lime, green apple, grapefruit*

OTHER *almonds, minerality*

ACIDITY *medium-high*

PAIRINGS

Vermentino goes well with fresh, herby foods.

TRY IT WITH

Pesto pasta salad

Shrimp scampi

A summer picnic

ITALIAN VERMENTINO MAY ALSO BE LABELED AS FAVORITA OR PIGATO.

Vermentino is widely grown throughout

Italy

On the Italian island of Sardinia, Vermentino takes on a fruitier, sometimes saline character.

This grape is also grown in

southern France

(although they call it "Rolle"). Vermentino from Corsica, France, often has subtle notes of minerality and smokiness.

RIESLING

—

Known for its floral aromas, good **RIESLING** can age for decades—many of the world's most expensive white wines are made from Riesling.

PRIMARY CHARACTERISTICS

FRUIT   *apricot, nectarine, peach, apple, pear*

- -

OTHER   *honey, ginger, citrus blossom*

- -

ACIDITY *high*

PAIRINGS

A sweet, acidic Riesling stands up well to spicy foods. Drink it with some Indian or Asian food, or try it with roasted vegetables like carrots, red onions and bell peppers.

TRY IT WITH

Spiced duck leg

Sesame chicken

Kung fu movie night

IF YOU WANT A DRY RIESLING, LOOK FOR ONE
WITH AN ABV OF AT LEAST 12.5 PERCENT.

Rieslings from	Rieslings from

Germany & California

France & Austria & Washington

tend to be sweet, but dry ones
are labeled "Trocken."

tend to be dry.

MOSCATO

—

One of the most popular wines produced from Muscat grapes is Moscato d'Asti—this lightly sparkling, low-alcohol wine (usually about 5.5 percent) is best served cold to help temper its sweetness.

PRIMARY CHARACTERISTICS

FRUIT   *peach, pear, lemon*

- -

OTHER   *honeysuckle, orange blossom*

- -

ACIDITY *medium-high*

PAIRINGS

This sweet wine is balanced nicely with spiced, aromatic Asian foods, or even just something a little salty.

TRY IT WITH

Vindaloo curry

Crispy pork belly

A summer pool party

MOSCATO IS THE ITALIAN NAME FOR MUSCAT BLANC GRAPES, WHICH COME IN MANY VARIETIES.

For a sweet, fortified (aka higher alcohol) Moscato, try a Muscat de Beaumes-de-Venise from

France's southern Rhône Valley.

If you want to try a drier version of Moscato, look for a bottle of "Secco" (dry) Moscato.

GEWÜRZTRAMINER

—

A classic example of aromatic wine, **GEWÜRZTRAMINER** (pronounced *"Geh-VERTZ-tram-eener"*) is low-acid, relatively rich and frequently has a very intense nose of fruits, flowers and spices.

PRIMARY CHARACTERISTICS

FRUIT *lychee, grapefruit, apricot*

OTHER *rose, ginger, warm spices*

ACIDITY *medium-low*

PAIRINGS

Gewürztraminer is best paired with foods that reinforce its floral and ginger notes.

TRY IT WITH

Garlic ginger chicken

Muenster cheese

A big blanket and your favorite sitcom

IN GERMAN, *GEWÜRZ* MEANS "SPICE," A REFERENCE TO THE WINE'S SPICY AROMAS.

Though the grape is thought to be German in origin, the majority of Gewürztraminer is produced in

France's Alsace region.

When buying U.S. Gewürztraminer, look for bottles from

New York or Washington,

or cooler climates in

California, like Sonoma.

CHENIN BLANC

—

CHENIN BLANC can range from dry to sweet depending on the winemaker's style and how ripe the grapes were when harvested.

PRIMARY CHARACTERISTICS

FRUIT *yellow apple, pear, lime*

OTHER *lemon, ginger, honey, saffron*

ACIDITY *medium-high*

PAIRINGS

Chenin Blanc's relatively high acidity and sweet notes make it a good choice for pairing with sweet and sour dishes.

TRY IT WITH

| Cheese and fruit plate | Sweet and sour pork | Eating al fresco |

GENERALLY, FRENCH CHENIN BLANC IS AROMATIC, WHILE SOUTH AFRICAN "STEEN" IS MORE CRISP.

Chenin Blanc is the most widely grown grape in

South Africa

where many winemakers are bottling easy-drinking wines with notes of stone fruit. You might see it called "Steen" on the label.

Chenin Blanc is also famously produced in

Vouvray

a region in France's Loire Valley.

CHARDONNAY

—

Aging **CHARDONNAY** in oak barrels gives the wine notes of vanilla and butter, while a process called malolactic fermentation is responsible for its smooth, creamy texture.

PRIMARY CHARACTERISTICS

FRUIT *lemon, pear, apple, passionfruit*

OTHER *honey, vanilla, butter*

ACIDITY *medium-low*

PAIRINGS

Pair an oaky Chardonnay with light, simply prepared foods that won't overwhelm the wine's flavors.

TRY IT WITH

Shrimp and grits

White pizza

A fall foliage train ride

LEGEND HAS IT REDS STAINED CHARLEMAGNE'S BEARD, UPSETTING HIS WIFE, SO HE ONLY DRANK CHARDONNAY.

Oaked Chardonnays are generally produced in warmer regions like

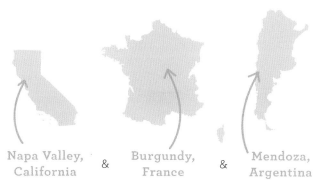

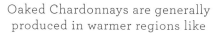

Napa Valley, California   &   Burgundy, France   &   Mendoza, Argentina

For a more crisp and minerally Chardonnay, look for an unoaked bottle from cooler regions like California's Sonoma Coast or France's Chablis region.

SÉMILLON

—

This grape is often found in expensive blends like white Bordeaux, but single varietal **SÉMILLON** wines are usually great value bottles in the U.S.

PRIMARY CHARACTERISTICS

FRUIT   *citrus, apple, mango*

OTHER   *honey, wax, ginger*

ACIDITY *medium*

PAIRINGS

Sémillon's fuller body and fresh flavors make it a good choice for extremely flavorful dishes.

TRY IT WITH

Sushi

Tandoori chicken

A summer sunset

THIS GRAPE IS FAMOUS FOR BEING BLENDED WITH SAUVIGNON BLANC IN SAUTERNES DESSERT WINES.

Sémillon from warmer climates like

California & Argentina

& South Africa

tend to have more tropical fruit flavors and buttery notes.

When produced in cooler climates like

Bordeaux & Washington

Sémillon tends to have a slightly higher acidity and more floral notes.

VIOGNIER

If you're a fan of Chardonnay, you should definitely try **VIOGNIER**, a dry wine known for its extremely peachy notes.

PRIMARY CHARACTERISTICS

FRUIT *peach, tangerine, mango*

- -

OTHER *rose, vanilla, honey*

- -

ACIDITY *medium-low*

PAIRINGS

Viognier makes a full-bodied white wine that typically carries a lot of fruit with some more delicate notes, making it a good pairing for both spicy and mild fare.

TRY IT WITH

Cajun chicken

Tea sandwiches

A garden party

SOME SYRAH-BASED WINES WILL ADD A SMALL AMOUNT OF VIOGNIER TO BALANCE OUT THE RED.

Viognier originated in southern France, but a decent bottle from the Rhône Valley can be fairly expensive—if you do decide to treat yo'self, look for a bottle of "Condrieu."

Still tasty yet more affordable bottles of Viognier can be found from

southern Australia & U.S.

SPARKLING WINE

Sparkling wine is bubbly and fun, but if you think it's just for parties, think again! Effervescent wines can and should be consumed at pretty much any time. Mimosas, anyone?

CHAMPAGNE   PROSECCO   MOSCATO D'ASTI

There are actually several different methods for adding bubbles to sparkling wine.
The two most common ways are the "traditional" method (used for Champagne and Cava, among others) and the "tank" method (used for Prosecco and Lambrusco). Both use a second fermentation (by adding more yeast and sugar into the wine) as a means to trap CO_2—only inexpensive bulk sparkling wines are still wines that have been carbonated by machine.

The shape of your glass has a more noticeable effect when you're drinking sparkling wine.
A classic flute will help the bubbles last longest, making it ideal for brut Champagne, while a tulip glass helps capture the aromas, making it preferred for fruitier sparkling wines, like Prosecco and Cava. A coupe glass is a fun, retro choice that will make the bubbles disperse more quickly—try this one for a sweet sparkling wine, like Moscato d'Asti or Brachetto d'Acqui.

Sparkling wine should be served well-chilled, between 43 to 50 degrees F. You can either chill it for 2½ hours in the fridge, 20 to 25 minutes in the freezer or 10 minutes in an ice bucket. If you go for the ice bucket method, add water! This creates more surface contact with the wine bottle, chilling it faster.

Higher pressure wines will have finer bubbles and be labeled as sparkling, Mousseux, Crémant, Espumoso, Sekt or Spumante.
Wines bottled with less pressure will be labeled semi-sparkling, Frizzante, Spritzig, Pétillant or Pearl.

How to Open Sparkling Wine
1. Remove the foil. Loosen and remove the wire cage.
2. Immediately place your palm over the top of the cork, keeping it in place.
3. Hold the bottle at a 30-degree angle. Slowly turn the bottle, not the cork.
4. Ease the cork slowly out of the bottle.
[Technical editor's note: The releasing gas pressure should sound like a quiet *"phut."* You're going for an angel's fart rather than a loud pop.]

CHAMPAGNE

Only made in the **CHAMPAGNE** region of France, this wine is pricey because of the technique used to make it and the high market demand. Sparkling wines from other regions in France are known as "Crémant."

PRIMARY CHARACTERISTICS

FRUIT   *citrus, peach, white cherry*

- -

OTHER   *almond, toast*

- -

BODY   *medium*

- -

TANNIN *low*

- -

ACIDITY *high*

PAIRINGS

Champagne's high acidity makes it preferable to drink alongside food, which might be why a lot of people who only drink it for a toast or with wedding cake (one of the few foods it doesn't go well with) say they don't like Champagne.

TRY IT WITH

Lobster   Popcorn   An air of superiority

PROSECCO

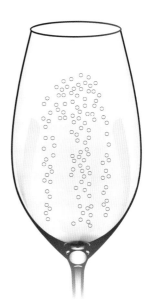

A more casual, less expensive sparkling wine than Champagne (but no less fun to drink), **PROSECCO** is made from Glera grapes and produced in the Veneto region of Italy.

PRIMARY CHARACTERISTICS

FRUIT	*green apple, honeydew, pear*
OTHER	*cream, honeysuckle*
BODY	*medium*
TANNIN	*low*
ACIDITY	*medium*

PAIRINGS

Just like Champagne, Prosecco goes well with a wide variety of foods.

TRY IT WITH

Drunken noodles   A charcuterie board   Sunday brunch

CAVA

Produced in Spain, **CAVA** is often less sweet than Prosecco and tastes closer to Champagne, making it an excellent value-buy for bubbly. The name "Cava" does not refer to a region or grape, but is a reference to the caves the wine was originally stored in.

PRIMARY CHARACTERISTICS

FRUIT *citrus, stone fruits, apple*

OTHER *chamomile, toasted nuts*

BODY *medium*

TANNIN *low*

ACIDITY *medium*

PAIRINGS

A dry Cava is perfect for cutting through creamy, fried or otherwise rich foods.

TRY IT WITH

Artichoke dip

Spanish tapas

An afternoon siesta

LAMBRUSCO

This sparkling red from northern Italy used to have a bad rap when cheap, overly sweet versions were popular in the 1970s and '80s, but quality bottles are making a comeback.

PRIMARY CHARACTERISTICS

FRUIT   *cherry, blackberry*

OTHER   *violet, cream*

BODY   *light-medium*

TANNIN *low-medium*

ACIDITY *medium-high*

PAIRINGS

While it pairs well with a wide range of foods, many choose to sip this easy-drinking wine alongside more casual fare.

TRY IT WITH

Grilled tuna

Fresh berries

A pizza party

DESSERT WINES

While there are some dry wines that can be enjoyed with dessert, "dessert wines" are a category of sweet, typically rich wines that are a perfect match for—or can be had as—an after-dinner treat.

FORTIFIED WINES

Fortified wines are wines that have been literally fortified, or strengthened, with alcohol. Usually, that alcohol is brandy. The process began as a way for explorers to keep their wine from spoiling on long ship voyages. Today we mostly keep doing it because it tastes good. But don't let that stop you from circumnavigating the globe with a few cases of the good stuff.

Sherry
Made in Spain, this fortified wine comes in a variety of styles. Dry Sherry may have notes of citrus and almond or chocolate and toffee, while sweet styles often have fig-like flavors.

Port
This fortified wine from Portugal is always sweet and usually red. For red fruit flavors with chocolate notes, look for a Ruby Port; for a nuttier version, try a bottle of Tawny Port.

Madeira
Madeira can be dry or sweet, often with notes of dried fruit, nuts, honey and smoke. Once opened, it lasts weeks or even months in the refrigerator before the flavors fade.

NOBLE ROT

This sounds gross but tastes delicious: Some of the world's best-loved dessert wines are made from grapes which have developed a very certain kind of fungus, drying them out and leaving behind super sweet pulp, creating wines that often have notes of ginger and honey. Two famous examples are SAUTERNES from BORDEAUX and TOKAJI from HUNGARY.

ICE WINE (EISWEIN)

Because of the unique circumstances required to produce this extremely sweet wine (the vineyard must have frozen over and the grapes must be pressed while still frozen), ice wine is hard to come by and a bit pricey. For obvious reasons, ice wine is most commonly made in CANADA, GERMANY and AUSTRIA.

DRIED GRAPE WINES

These highly sweet dessert wines are made from grapes that have been left out to dry and then pressed, essentially producing raisin juice as opposed to grape juice. VIN SANTO, one of the more famous examples of this wine, is traditionally paired with biscotti—some people even dip the hard cookies directly into the wine.

Dry to Sweet

Some dry wine grapes can be produced in sweeter styles that are also considered dessert wines. Some common examples are the wines in the Aromatic Whites section (see page 74). Red examples in this book include Schiava and Lambrusco (pages 54 and 93).

Perfect Pairings

Food and dessert wine pairings can be the most "eye-opening," according to Courtney Schiessl. As she explains it: "If you like tiramisu and you pair it with Marsala or with another kind of nutty dessert wine, it completely changes what the wine tastes like. It's totally not that sweet and it's way drier."

Media Lab Books
For inquiries, call 646-838-6637

Copyright 2019 Topix Media Lab

Published by Topix Media Lab
14 Wall Street, Suite 4B
New York, NY 10005

Printed in China

ISBN-13: 978-1-948174-10-7
ISBN-10: 1-948174-10-3

33614081398306

CEO Tony Romando

Vice President & Publisher Phil Sexton
Senior Vice President of Sales & New Markets Tom Mifsud
Vice President of Retail Sales & Logistics Linda Greenblatt
Director of Finance Vandana Patel
Manufacturing Director Nancy Puskuldjian
Financial Analyst Matthew Quinn

Editor-in-Chief Jeff Ashworth
Creative Director Steven Charny
Photo Director Dave Weiss
Managing Editor Courtney Kerrigan
Senior Editor Tim Baker

Content Designer Michelle Lock
Content Photo Editor Catherine Armanasco
Art Director Susan Dazzo
Assistant Managing Editor Holland Baker
Designer Danielle Santucci
Associate Editor Trevor Courneen
Copy Editor & Fact Checker Benjamin VanHoose

Co-Founders Bob Lee, Tony Romando